Charlie was a shepherd. He had
a cozy house, a big hat, a crook,
and a flock of fat sheep.

But everyone said,

"CHARLIE NEEDS A CLOAK"

story and pictures by

Tomie dePaola

FOR DUCHIN & FLORENCE ♡♡

Aladdin Paperbacks
An imprint of Simon & Schuster
Children's Publishing Division
1230 Avenue of the Americas
New York, N.Y. 10020
Text copyright © 1973 by Thomas dePaola
Manufactured in China
40
Library of Congress Cataloging-in-Publication Data
dePaola Thomas Anthony
"Charlie Needs a Cloak."
Summary: A Shepherd shears his sheep, cards and
spins the wool, weaves and dyes the cloth, and sews
a beautiful new red cloak.
1. Woolen and worsted manufacture-Juvenile literature.
2. Tailoring-Juvenile literature. [1. Wool. 2. Clothing
and dress] I. Title.
TS1626.D4 646.4'5 73-16365
ISBN 978-0-671-66467-1 (pbk)
0216 SCP

Poor Charlie!

He really needed a new cloak.

So, in the spring, Charlie sheared
his sheep.

He washed the wool,

and carded the wool to straighten
it out.

Then Charlie spun the wool into yarn.

Charlie wanted a red cloak, so he picked some pokeweed berries during the late summer, and boiled them over a fire.

Then Charlie dyed the yarn red
in the berry juice.

After the yarn was dry, Charlie put the strands on the loom.

And every fall evening, he wove the yarn into cloth.

Charlie put the cloth on the table
and cut it into pieces.

He pinned the pieces together,

and sewed them.

And then, when winter came,

Charlie had a beautiful new red cloak.

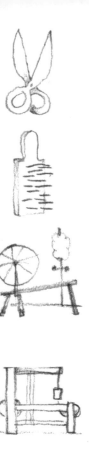

shear-To clip the wool from a sheep.

card-To untangle wool with a comb or brush.

spin-To twist wool into yarn.

weave-To twist thread into cloth.

sew-To fasten together with thread.

cloak-A coat without sleeves.